Money Management
Certification Program™

Online Software
Included

Created by:

A Complete *Step-by-Step* Program for Learning Money Management™

FamilyMint Publishing

www.familymint.com

Copyright © 2012 FamilyMint

Robert Masterson, MBA   *Jeff Eusebio, MBA*

About This Workbook

Your child needs a solid foundation to become money-smart. This workbook has been compiled and tested by a team of children's money management experts to increase your child's understanding, confidence, and success.

 Aligns to Jump$tart National Standards for K-12 Personal Finance Education

 Makes learning money management engaging and fun

 Develops foundational money management habits

 Easily and effectively teaches your kids to be money-smart

COMPUTER NOT NECESSARY

If you don't have access to the Internet, don't worry.
This workbook is complete and self-contained.

FM FamilyMint

FamilyMint.com is an award-winning online money management and goal-setting application that offers an engaging way for kids to learn financial responsibility. It's easy for kids to use, lets them connect their money with real-world meaning, and most importantly, learn by doing. It's available via both web and mobile interfaces.

Contributors and Supporters

Cornerstone Credit Union Foundation's mission is to empower people to improve their financial well being. Special thanks to CCUF for their help in funding the creation of this workbook.

The Youth Financial Literacy Foundation is a 501(c)3 non-profit organization whose mission is to start young people off with the advantage of a sound financial education.

Table of Contents

Online Software Access

Turn to **page 55** for instructions on accessing the online software.

We always like hearing from you. If you have any feedback or suggestions,
please email us at feedback@familymint.com.

Introduction

Introduction for Parents and Teachers

This program is designed to develop money management habits that will benefit children for the rest of their lives. It will help children form a firm base from which to launch solid financial literacy skills and habits.

> "The number one problem in today's generation and economy is the lack of financial literacy."
> - Alan Greenspan, Federal Reserve Chairman, 1987 to 2006

Financial success and independence starts with forming the right habits and behaviors. This workbook will help form and reinforce the following principles:

- saving money,
- tracking money,
- setting goals,
- delaying gratification,
- writing checks and deposit slips,
- budgeting,
- understanding interest,
- and more!

> **Note:**
>
> We recommend placing the child's money into an empty jar or coffee can that can be decorated and become the child's money vault.

The Parent Holds the Money

For the duration of this program, the parent or guardian will act as the "banker" and hold their child's money. This interaction is an important part of the learning experience, because it creates accountability between children and their money. Since the parent is acting as the banker, the child is forced to justify how he or she is spending his or her money. This may initially sound difficult or even unnecessary, but it has been proven to be highly effective in teaching money management to children. You'll find it's also a source of many new teachable moments. See the image on the next page to see how this process works.

If you chose not to act as the "banker", go into the Settings screen in the online software, and turn off the "Deposit Approval Required" and "Withdraw Approval Required" settings.

Workbook or Online?

The back section of this workbook contains the worksheets and forms your child can use to complete the program. You may prefer to skip using the worksheets and instead use the online version of FamilyMint to simulate today's online banking experience.

Introduction

To set this up, *the parent, not the child* needs to create an online family account. Refer to **page 55** to sign up. Create a user name and password for the child. After this, the child will log in and do all the work themselves! All the parent needs to do is monitor and approve. Review the online introduction video to get started after you sign up.

$ This symbol is used in the workbook any time FamilyMint online may be used in place of the worksheets in the book.

The image below explains how you will act as the "banker" for the duration of this program. When your child makes a deposit, he or she gives you the money. When your child makes a withdrawal, he or she gets his or her money back from you. The pictures below refer to FamilyMint online but your child can use the worksheets in this workbook just as effectively.

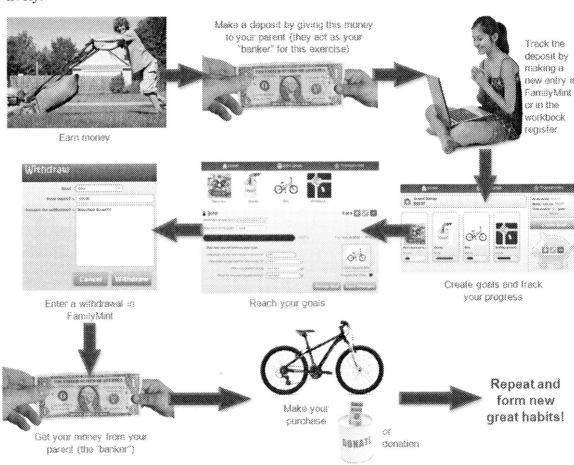

Earn money

Make a deposit by giving this money to your parent (they act as your "banker" for this exercise)

Track the deposit by making a new entry in FamilyMint or in the workbook register

Create goals and track your progress

Withdraw

Enter a withdrawal in FamilyMint

Reach your goals

Get your money from your parent (the "banker")

Make your purchase   or   donation

Repeat and form new great habits!

This program is designed to run for a period of at least two months in order to allow your child to practice the concepts learned and form the habits mentioned earlier.

Once your child has completed the workbook, present him or her with the Certificate of Achievement found at the back of the workbook. Cut this out and display it proudly!

Congratulations for focusing on financial literacy!

Instructions

How to use this program

Before getting started with the exercises in this workbook, ask your parent or guardian if they want you to use FamilyMint online or the worksheets at the back of this workbook. Whenever you see the FamilyMint coin, ⊚ it means you can use FamilyMint online rather than the worksheets within this workbook. The online version of FamilyMint will do all the calculations for you and give you an experience just like real online banking.

Now let's get started...

Step 1:

☐ Read the "Tracking Your Money" chapter and complete the exercises.

☐ Make an initial deposit with your virtual banker (your parent) and track the deposit as a transaction on the General Savings Tracking Worksheet. ⊚

☐ Start tracking all of your money coming in and going out on the General Savings Tracking Worksheet. ⊚

Step 2:

☐ Read the "Goal Setting" chapter and complete the exercises.

☐ Start tracking your top three goals using the Goal Tracking Worksheets. Make sure you create at least one goal that you believe you can achieve in the next eight weeks. ⊚

☐ At the end of the week, fill out the Net Worth / Total Balance worksheet.

Note:

This program is designed to allow you to complete the workbook at your pace. As a guideline, a chapter should take no more than one week.

Step 3:

☐ Read the "Budgeting" chapter and complete the exercises.

☐ Create your own virtual envelope system. ⑤

☐ At the end of the week, fill out the Net Worth / Total Balance worksheet.

Step 4:

☐ Read the "Interest—Growing $" chapter and complete the exercises.

☐ At the end of the week, fill out the Net Worth / Total Balance worksheet.

Step 5:

☐ Continue to track all of your money coming in and going out for a few more weeks. ⑤

☐ Continue to work hard toward achieving your goals.

☐ Achieve at least one of your goals. ⑤

☐ At the end of each week, fill out the Net Worth / Total Balance worksheet.

Wrap-Up:

☐ Complete the "Learning Summary".

☐ Have your parent fill out the Parent Checklist and sign the certificate.

☐ Celebrate what you've learned!

> **Note:**
>
> Tracking your money, setting goals, and planning for the future are lifelong habits. We encourage you to continue these after achieving your certification!

Why track your money?

Tracking your **money** is very important. It helps you understand:

- how much money you have now

- how much you are expecting in the future

- how you are spending your money now

- how much money you need for future expenses

This is called **money management**. It might seem like a lot of work, but it really isn't, especially if you make it a habit.

How much money do you have now? Count up all the money that you have in your wallet, purse, pockets, bedroom, and any where else and write it down below. You will write this number down as your starting balance in the Tracking Worksheet or in FamilyMint a little later.

All the money I have: $ ....

Income

You can receive money through many sources such as an **allowance**, part time jobs like babysitting, collecting deposits on empty cans or even as a gift. This is called **income**.

Fun Money Fact

Before the days of paper money, Americans traded animal skins, including deer and elk bucks, for goods and services. Hence the word "buck" to describe money.

 Take a minute and write down all the ways you have received money.

Income

example: babysitting	

Do you receive any of this income on a regular basis, such as a weekly allowance or money from a part time job? This is the money you can use to help guide your future spending. Put a star next to those recurring incomes.

Expenses

Expenses are things that you spend your money on. When it comes to money management, spending the money seems to be the easiest thing to do. But it's very important to keep track of where that money is going. There are certain expenses that happen on a regular basis like cell phone bills. What's good about regular expenses is you can plan for these things. But most expenses when you are young are those things that just come up out of the blue like going to a movie or buying a candy bar. These expenses can add up quickly.

Fun Money Fact

The largest bill ever printed was the $100,000 bill.

The $100 bill has been the largest denomination of currency in circulation since 1969.

 Now try and think of all the things you have purchased over the past year. If you have been tracking your expenses then this will be really easy. List some of the things that you spent your money on in the table below.

Expenses

example: snacks	

How to track your money

Vocabulary

Register – A written record of items, names or actions.

Transactions – The act of receiving or giving, buying or selling.

Deposit – Adding or placing money into an account.

Withdrawal – Taking money out of an account.

Balance – Amount of money in an account at any given time.

If you keep your money in a piggy bank and you take out $10 to go to a movie, how much money do you have left? Well, if you want to know, you'll have to take out all of the money and count it. Unless you write that number down, you will probably forget it. This means the next time you go to your piggy bank to take money out, you'll need to recount all of it again.   This is not a good way to keep track of your money!

Seeing where your money is coming from and where it is going to is key to money management. The best way to keep track of what's happening with your money is in a **register**. A register is simply a record of **transactions** or **deposits** and **withdrawals**.

A register shows you the date the transaction took place, what the transaction was for and how much it cost. Most importantly, it shows you how much money you have. This is called your **balance**. See the example below.

Workbook Register (*example*)

Date of transaction | Where the money came from or went | How much is subtracted or withdrawn | How much is added or deposited | How much money you have

DATE	DESCRIPTION	SUBTRACTIONS Amount of Payment	ADDITIONS Amount of Deposit	BALANCE
11/2	Starting Balance		$75.00	$75.00
11/7	Go to movies with friends	$10.00		$65.00
11/15	New video game	$35.00		$30.00
11/20	Gift from Aunt Karen		$25.00	$55.00
11/23	Allowance money		$2.00	$57.00

Doesn't this look like a better way of managing your money?   A register can either be in paper or electronic form.   An example of the FamilyMint online register where you log into

your FamilyMint account to manage your money is shown below. You input your transactions using your computer. The advantage here is that all the math is done for you.

FamilyMint online register (*example*)

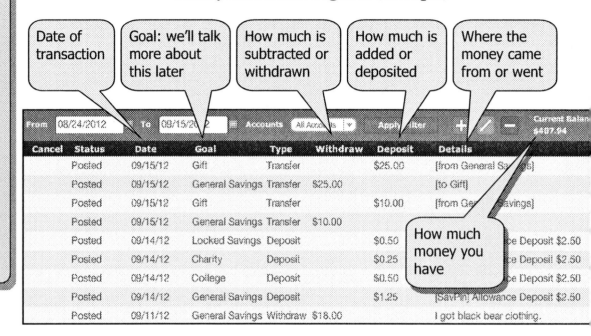

Date of transaction

Goal: we'll talk more about this later

How much is subtracted or withdrawn

How much is added or deposited

Where the money came from or went

How much money you have

Cancel	Status	Date	Goal	Type	Withdraw	Deposit	Details
	Posted	09/15/12	Gift	Transfer		$25.00	[from General Savings]
	Posted	09/15/12	General Savings	Transfer	$25.00		[to Gift]
	Posted	09/15/12	Gift	Transfer		$10.00	[from General Savings]
	Posted	09/15/12	General Savings	Transfer	$10.00		
	Posted	09/14/12	Locked Savings	Deposit		$0.50	...ce Deposit $2.50
	Posted	09/14/12	Charity	Deposit		$0.25	...ce Deposit $2.50
	Posted	09/14/12	College	Deposit		$0.50	...ce Deposit $2.50
	Posted	09/14/12	General Savings	Deposit		$1.25	[SavMin] Allowance Deposit $2.50
	Posted	09/11/12	General Savings	Withdraw	$18.00		I got black bear clothing.

Checks and deposit slips

When you are older, you might not always have the cash you need on hand to pay for something, so instead you may write a **check**. A check represents a withdrawal from the money that you have in your checking account.

When you pay for something with a check you are giving the store permission to take your check to a bank or credit union and exchange it for money. The amount of money you wrote the check for will be withdrawn from your checking account. So you need to make sure you have the money in your account to cover the check. This is another reason why tracking your money by keeping a register up-to-date is so important!

Deposit slips are included in the back of a **checkbook** and are used when making a deposit into your checking account. Deposit slips contain much of the same information as checks. Even though you may have a few years before you will have your own checking account, it's never too early to understand this very important concept.

Fun Money Fact

On April 2, 1792, Congress created the U. S. Mint. A month later, land was purchased for its construction in Philadelphia, which was then the nation's capital.

How checks work

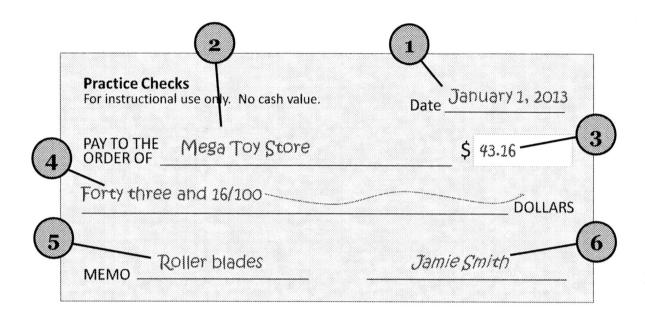

Now let's take a closer look at a check and how you fill in each of the parts.

1. <u>Date</u> the check is filled out

2. <u>Who</u> the check is written out to -- a person or a business.

3. <u>Amount owed</u> written out as numbers

4. <u>Amount owed</u> written out as words starting at the far left side with the cents written as a fraction (42/100) followed by a squiggly line

    So why do you have to write the amount twice? This serves two purposes:

    -   First, seeing it written both ways helps avoid confusion. When you write something out, you are forced to think about what you are doing rather than if you just write some numbers down.

    -   The second reason is that it helps prevent someone from changing the amount. You certainly don't want someone adding a one to the beginning or a zero to the end, do you?

5. <u>Description</u> of what the check is for.

6. <u>Signature</u> saying you wrote the check and agree to have the money withdrawn from your checking account.

Ready to practice? Turn the page to practice filling in a check on your own.

Fill in the check on the next page. Pretend you are buying a pair of shoes at Shoe World and the shoes cost $27.45. Refer back here if you need help.

Fun Money Fact

Some experts believe the first check was invented by the Ancient Romans around 352 BC, but checks did not gain wide use until the 1700s in England.

Practice Checks
For instructional use only. No cash value.

Date _____

PAY TO THE
ORDER OF _____ $ [   ]

_____ DOLLARS

MEMO _____ _____

Let's take a closer look at a deposit slip and each of its parts.

How deposit slips work

1. <u>Date</u> the deposit slip is filled out

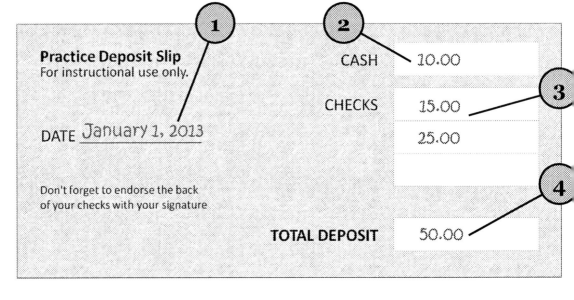

Fun Money Fact

A mile of pennies laid out is worth $844.80. By this standard, America is about $2.5 million wide, coast-to-coast.

Practice Deposit Slip
For instructional use only.

① ②

CASH   10.00

CHECKS   15.00   ③
              25.00

DATE January 1, 2013

Don't forget to endorse the back
of your checks with your signature

④

TOTAL DEPOSIT   50.00

2. <u>Amount of Cash</u> to be deposited

3. <u>Amount of each Check</u> to be deposited - checks are listed individually

4. <u>Total amount</u> being deposited - add up all of the checks and cash

Fill in the deposit on the next page. Pretend you are depositing the following:

Answer Key

 Find the answers to exercises on page 53

- Cash = $25.00
- Check 1 = $10.00
- Check 2 = $30.00
- Check 3 = $20.00

Practice Deposit Slip
For instructional use only.

CASH

CHECKS

DATE _____

SIGNATURE _____

TOTAL DEPOSIT

Vocabulary

Endorse – The placing of your signature on a document.

I know what you're thinking. What if you have more than three checks to deposit? Great question! The deposit slips at your credit union or bank have more room on the back to add additional checks. Don't forget to **endorse** the back of your checks.

So now you have a good idea about how checks and deposit slips work and how to fill them out. Turn to ***page 44*** for additional practice checks and deposit slips.

 You've learned a lot of new vocabulary. Now try matching the vocabulary word with the correct definition. Draw a line from the word to its definition.

- Transaction
- Money Management
- Income
- Register
- Check
- Deposit
- Endorse
- Withdrawal

- A written record of items, names or actions
- Adding or placing money into an account
- A form of payment that is withdrawn from your account
- The placing of one's signature on a document
- Process of tracking income, savings and spending
- Taking money out of an account
- The act of receiving or giving, buying or selling
- Money received

Assignment

Now it's time to start tracking your real money! Your parent is going to act as the banker and will hold on to your money.

Getting started:

1. Find an empty coffee can or jar and personalize it with your name, stickers or whatever you want. This is going to be your *"money vault"* while you complete this program.

2. Place all the money you counted up earlier into your "money vault".

3. Now it's time to fill out your first deposit slip on *page 49*.

4. This next step is the most important! You must write down the amount of money you just deposited with the description **Starting Balance** using either:

   - FamilyMint online. Log in to your account and click on the deposit button, or

   - The General Savings Tracking Worksheets starting on *page 28*

> **Note:**
> - If your parent / guardian hasn't set up an online FamilyMint account, have them refer to *page 1* to get started.
> - For additional help in tracking money within FamilyMint, go to *support.familymint.com*

Hurray! You've made your first deposit and you're on your way towards successful money management!

5. Whenever you wish to spend your money, just make a withdrawal transaction on your worksheets or online using FamilyMint.

6. Whenever you receive or make any money, just make a deposit transaction on your worksheets or online using FamilyMint.

Continued learning *(optional)*

Write a check whenever you wish to make a withdrawal. Make the check out to the place of business you are making the purchase from, but give the check to your parent. *Remember, you can only write a check when you have enough money in your account to cover it.* When you wish to make a deposit, fill out a deposit slip. For additional practice checks and deposit slips, go to **www.familymint.com/forms**.

What is a goal?

A **goal** is something you want to achieve that requires effort on your part. There may be many things that you want, but if you don't work to make them happen, they are nothing more than a dream or a wish.

Did you know only three percent of people set goals? Why don't more people set goals? Because setting goals is hard. It means you may have to make tough choices about how you spend your money and your time. But that doesn't mean you shouldn't try.

Let's look at a real life example of someone who set a goal and didn't give up until he achieved it.

Goal of reinventing the vacuum cleaner - James Dyson, inventor of the first vacuum cleaner without a bag is a perfect example of someone who had a goal and saw it through to the end. Seeing a problem with traditional vacuum suction, James Dyson made it his goal to develop a better solution. While visiting a saw mill he noticed that the sawdust was removed from the air by large industrial cyclones, which are like tornados with very fast rotating wind. He wondered if this same idea could work on a smaller scale. James Dyson created over 5,000 working prototypes through trial and error before he finally got it right. You might ask why anyone would keep doing something if they continued to fail. Well, James Dyson had a goal and a vision and saw each failure as bringing him one step closer to his goal. He achieved his goal and his new design has revolutionized the vacuum industry.

Wow! What an amazing story! Can you see how important it is to have goals? Imagine if James Dyson didn't have a goal or gave up after attempt 4,999. Sometimes achieving a goal may seem very difficult, but the end result of achieving your goal is well worth the effort.

Goals are self-fulfilling, create energy, and can lead to incredible lives. The first step to success is having a goal.

Secrets to achieving goals

Secret #1: Write it down!

 If you write down your goals, you are far more likely to achieve them. So let's make some goals! Take a few minutes and think about some things that you would really like to do with your money. Maybe your goal is a bike, a new video game, or donating to a charity or cause that is important to you. Write your goals down below.

My Goals

example: New Bike

Secret #2: Make SMART goals!

There are some simple rules to help you achieve your goals. We remember these rules with the acronym SMART! SMART goals take goals to the next level and give you something you can really sink your teeth into. SMART stands for:

S	= Specific	Specific means you have a clear goal in mind. Wanting to buy a gift for your mom is not specific. Wanting to buy red roses is specific.
M	= Measurable	How much do red roses cost?
A	= Achievable	Is it realistic that you can accomplish the goal you wish to achieve? Buying three red roses is a more realistic goal to achieve than buying 100 red roses.
R	= Relevant	Saving to buy your mom wrenches that she would never use doesn't make sense. Choose goals that matter.
T	= Time-bound	When do you want to want to buy these roses? If it's for your mom's birthday which is two months away, then you can begin to plan how you will save for those roses.

Fun Money Fact

Did you know that a quarter has 119 grooves around the edge, and a dime has 118?

 Now for practice let's take one of the goals you just created and create a SMART goal. Pick one of the goals that you believe you can accomplish in the next couple of months. Fill in the SMART table below.

		Example	*Your Goal*
S	= **S**pecific	*3 Red Roses*	
M	= **M**easurable	*$6.00*	
A	= **A**chievable	*Yes*	
R	= **R**elevant	*Yes*	
T	= **T**ime-bound	*June 20*	

Secret #3: Do something every day!

Now that you have a SMART goal written down you need to break it down into smaller chunks. *How do you eat an elephant? One bite at a time.*

Doing something small every day is a great way to build the discipline you need to succeed, especially as your goals get bigger.

Break your goals down into bite-sized chunks!

> Using our three red roses gift example, let's say the cost is $6 and you want to purchase them in four weeks. By dividing $6 by four, you need to save $1.50 per week. If you break it down by day, you only need to save a quarter a day. When you break a goal down like this you start to see how manageable it really can be.

If you fall behind, don't get discouraged. Just get right back in there and keep plugging away until you reach your goal. That's why you wrote it down, so it's always in front of you.

Assignment

Remember the goals you wrote down earlier? Let's track the top three or four goals by using either:

- FamilyMint online. After you log on, just click the **Create Goal** button and fill in the blanks, OR

- the Goal Tracking Worksheets starting on *page 32*.

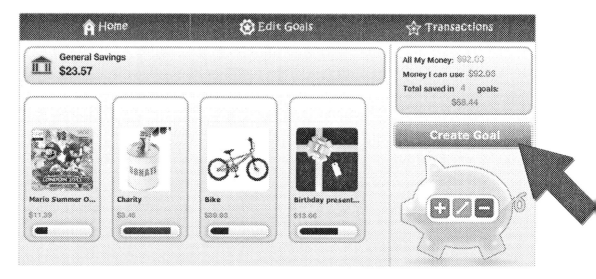

Either way you are going to be practicing the three secrets to achieving goals!

Note:

- *For additional help in setting up goals within FamilyMint, go to* ___support.familymint.com___

3 | Budgeting

Budgeting Using the Envelope System

So far you've learned how to track your money and set SMART goals. Now you are going to learn how creating a **budget** is the secret to achieving your goals one step at a time.

You're going to learn a simple but very effective method of budgeting called the **envelope system**. This system has been around for ages and for good reason – it works! The envelope system works like this: you decide up front how much of each dollar you earn is going towards each of your savings goals. Hmmm, that sounded a bit complicated, didn't it? It's not! Let's explain further with an example.

Let's say you really want to achieve three goals: (1) a new game, (2) new shoes, and (3) giving to the fundraiser at school. With these goals in mind you set up three envelopes to contain the money that you are saving toward each of these goals. You would just write the name of each goal on the envelope like this:

Now let's say that you make $10 washing cars. Are you going to go blow that $10 on candy and a movie? No way! Not if you ever want to achieve your goals. Instead, you smartly decide to divide that $10 between each of your goals. But, you have to be realistic at the same time, and know that little things like buying candy or going to the movies are things you'll also want to spend your money on. So you decide you want to keep part of your money for other purchases. You call this 4th envelope General Savings, because it's savings for "general stuff". Perhaps you divide up your $10 like this:

- 20% will go toward your new Game

- 20% will go towards your new Shoes

- 10% will go toward your school Fundraiser

- and the remaining 50% will go into General Savings

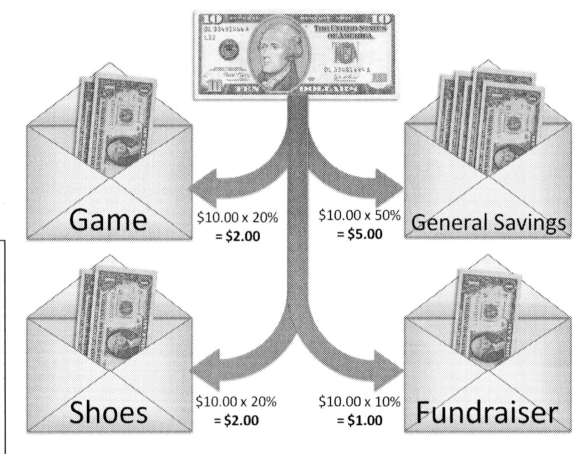

Fun Money Fact

The lifespan of a $1 bill is about 22 months. The lifespan gets longer for the larger bills because they are used less frequently.

And that's the envelope system—deciding up front how much of each dollar is going to each of your goals!

 Now that you've learned what the envelope system is and have seen an example of how to use it, try it yourself.

You just received $40.00 for your birthday and you want to deposit this into your envelopes according to the same percentages you saw in the previous example. Calculate how much money should go into each envelope and write the answers in the blanks below:

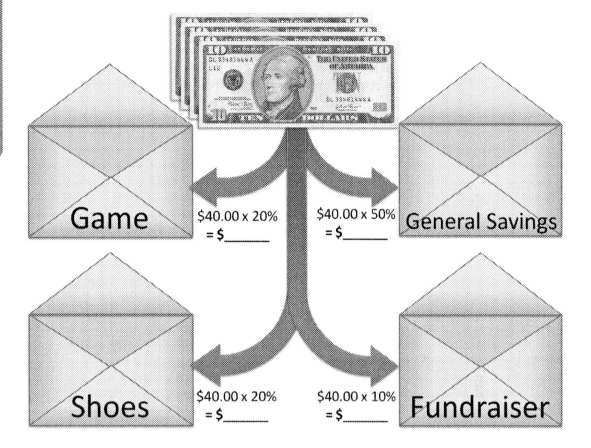

Game $40.00 x 20% = $_____ $40.00 x 50% = $_____ General Savings

Shoes $40.00 x 20% = $_____ $40.00 x 10% = $_____ Fundraiser

Assignment

Vocabulary

Allocate - To assign for a particular purpose.

Saving Plan - FamilyMint's version of the envelope system.

With this program, you are going to be tracking your money either online or with worksheets. You will use "virtual" envelopes to **allocate** your money rather than using real envelopes. These virtual envelopes are the General Savings and Goal Tracking Worksheets!

Now, pick two or three of the goals you made earlier and create your own virtual envelopes including the percentages you will use to split up your deposits. You can do this either (1) online or (2) using the table below:

1. If you use FamilyMint online, the envelope system savings process is automated for you. It's called the **"Savings Plan"**. Log in to FamilyMint online, click on Savings Plan, and fill out the Savings Allocation column.

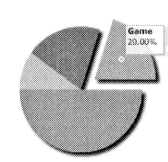

Account	Locked	Matching	Savings Allocation
General Savings			50%
Game	🔓	0%	20
Shoes	🔓	0%	20
Fundraiser	🔓	0%	10

Reminder

When dividing your money by percentages, remember that all the percentages have to add up to 100%. *For example:*

20%
30%
40%
+10%
100%

2. If you are not using FamilyMint online, fill out the table below with the percentages you've decided to allocate to each goal.

Goal	Percentage

Continued learning *(optional)*

Now that you've created your own envelope system, start using it for each of your deposits. If you use FamilyMint online, select Savings Plan when you make a deposit. If you are using the workbook, do the calculations manually just like you did in the exercise on the previous page, and then make the deposit entries in each of the Goal and General Savings Worksheets.

What is interest?

Vocabulary

Principal – The original sum of money before any interest is added.

Interest – A charge for the privilege of borrowing money. This charge is typically figured on an annual or yearly basis.

Lend – Allowing a person or organization the use of a sum of money under an agreement to pay it back later, typically with interest.

Imagine you want to buy your first car. Do you have $20,000 in your piggy bank? Probably not. So you will need to borrow some money from your credit union or bank. When they lend you money so you can buy a car, you are agreeing to pay the original money borrowed, known as the **principal**, plus additional money that has been agreed to, known as **interest**. Well, the same is true when you deposit your money into a savings account. You are lending your money to the bank or credit union and they are agreeing to pay you interest on your money while they hold it.

There are two types of interest that you can earn; **simple interest** and **compound interest**. Simple interest is money added only to the starting principal. For example, let's say you lend someone $100, which would be the principal. The person agrees to pay a simple annual interest rate of 10% and the principle is to be paid back in five years. To figure out how much money is owed to you at the end of the five years, use the following formula:

Simple Interest = Principal x Interest Rate x Number of Years

= $100 x 10% x 5 = $50

Another way to look at it is by showing what happens year-by-year as shown below.

Simple Interest *(Example)*

Principal = $100	Current Balance	Interest Paid = 10%	Principal + Interest
Year 1	*$100.00*	$10.00	$110.00
Year 2	*$110.00*	$10.00	$120.00
Year 3	*$120.00*	$10.00	$130.00
Year 4	*$130.00*	$10.00	$140.00
Year 5	*$140.00*	$10.00	$150.00
	Total Int.	**$50.00**	

The next type of interest is compound interest. This is the type of interest you earn when you deposit your money in the credit union or bank. Albert Einstein called compound interest the "eighth wonder of the world." Compound interest works like magic, with your money constantly feeding on itself to grow larger and larger. How does it work? It's easy really. Interest is earned and paid not just on your principal, but also on all the previous interest earned. Your total balance grows faster and faster without you doing a thing!

Using the same example we did with simple interest, let's now apply it to compound interest. The formula for compound interest looks like this:

Compound Interest = [Principal x (1 + Interest Rate) [# of Years]**] - Principal**

$$= [\$100 \times (1+0.10)^5] - \$100$$

Number of years is an **exponent** because you multiply the math equation within the parenthesis this many times. This may sound confusing, so let's demonstrate using our above example.

$$= [\$100 \times (1+0.10)^5] - \$100$$

$$= [\$100 \times (1.10 \times 1.10 \times 1.10 \times 1.10 \times 1.10)] - \$100$$

$$= (\$100 \times 1.6105) - \$100$$

$$= \mathbf{\$61.05}$$

> ## Vocabulary
>
> **Exponent** – The exponent of a number shows you how many times the number is to be used in a multiplication. It is written as a small number to the right and above the base number.

> ## Reminder
>
> When there are multiple operations like in our compound interest example, we use parenthesis ( ) to tell us what operation to do first. The rule of thumb is to work from the inside out.

The table below shows how our money grows with compound interest year-by-year.

Compound Interest *(Example)*

Principal = $100	Current Balance	Interest Paid = 10%	Principal + Interest
Year 1	*$100.00*	*$10.00*	*$110.00*
Year 2	*$110.00*	*$11.00*	*$121.00*
Year 3	*$121.00*	*$12.10*	*$133.10*
Year 4	*$133.10*	*$13.31*	*$146.41*
Year 5	*$146.41*	*$14.64*	*$161.05*
	Total Int.	***$61.05***	

Compound interest has given us an extra **$11.05** on the same $100 over five years compared to simple interest. Pretty cool, huh? Compound interest is one of the secrets of putting your money to work for you. Let's see the simple and compound interest example compared side by side.

> ### Note:
>
> *Notice how your current balance goes up every year. Unlike with simple interest, you are being paid interest on the entire growing balance.*

Principal = $100	Simple Interest	Compound Interest
Year 1	$10.00	$10.00
Year 2	$10.00	$11.00
Year 3	$10.00	$12.10
Year 4	$10.00	$13.31
Year 5	$10.00	$14.64
Total Int.	**$50.00**	**$61.05**

Answer Key

Find the answers to exercises on page 54

Exercises

Solve the following problems to find the simple and compound interests.

1. If you deposit **$500** into an account paying you **10% <u>simple</u> interest**, how much will earn in **5 years**? *Refer to example on page 21 for help.*

    (a) Calculate the answer using the simple interest formula:

    Simple Interest = Principal x Interest Rate x Number of Years

    Solve Here

    (b) Calculate the answer using the table below. Remember, with simple interest, the current year's interest is calculated based on the **Principal**, not the Current Balance.

Principal = $500	Current Balance	Interest Paid = 10%	Principal + Interest
Year 1	$	$	$
Year 2	$	$	$
Year 3	$	$	$
Year 4	$	$	$
Year 5	$	$	$
Total Int.	$		

Reminder

Refer back to pages **21** and **22** for examples on how to complete the exercises.

Refer to page **19** for help on percentages.

You can use a calculator for these exercise if you like.

Parents

Feel free to work with your child on these problems. By completing these problems, your child will begin to understand the power of interest.

2. If you deposit **$500** into an account paying you **10% <u>compound</u> interest**, how much will you earn in **5 years**? *Refer to example on page 22 for help.*

    (a) Calculate the answer using the compound interest formula:

    Compound Interest = [Principal x (1 + Interest Rate)$^{\text{# of Years}}$] - Principal

    Solve Here

Turn page and fill in the table.

Exercises

(b) Calculate the answer using the table below. Remember, with compound interest, the current year's interest is calculated based on the **Current Balance**, not the Principal.

Principal = $500	Current Balance	Interest Paid = 10%	Principal + Interest
Year 1	$	$	$
Year 2	$	$	$
Year 3	$	$	$
Year 4	$	$	$
Year 5	$	$	$
	Total Int.	$	

3. How much more did you earn with compound interest as compared to simple interest?

Compound Interest Earned:_____

-    Simple Interest Earned:_____

=   Difference:_____

Continued learning *(optional)*

Within the FamilyMint application, the parent can set up interest that can automatically be paid on a weekly or monthly basis. Since this is a two month program, we recommend an interest rate of 10%, and having it paid weekly so your child can see the impact of interest on their savings.

*Go to **support.familymint.com** for help setting up automated interest in FamilyMint.*

Use stacks of pennies to visually show how compound interest works. Start with 10 pennies in a stack. This is your starting principal and you will earn 10% interest per year. Year two will have 11 pennies (10 principal + 1 interest). Year three will have 12 pennies (11 + 1) and so on. Remember this is compound interest, so soon you'll be adding more than one penny per year (round for simplicity). After 10 years notice how you have more than doubled your money! How tall would the stack of pennies be after 20 years?

Fun Money Fact

If you have three quarters, four dimes and four pennies, you have $1.19. You also have the largest amount of money in coins possible without being able to make change for a dollar

---

Learning Summary

Wrap-Up

1. What have you learned as a result of completing this program?
Write down what you've learned. Cover these areas:

a.) Tracking your money

b.) Setting goals

c.) Budgeting

d.) Interest

2. It takes several weeks to form new habits. Write down an example of how your money management habits have changed as a result of completing this program.

Worksheets & Forms

About This Section

Use the worksheets in this section to help complete your money management certification. These worksheets include:

- $ • General Savings Tracking Worksheet

- $ • Goal Tracking Worksheets

- $ • Net Worth / Total Balance Worksheet

- • Checks

- • Deposit Slips

$ ***FamilyMint Online:*** *You can use FamilyMint online (www.familymint.com) to track all of your money electronically instead of using these worksheets. If you do use FamilyMint online, you won't need to manually fill out the General Savings Tracking Worksheet, the Goal Tracking Worksheet, or the Net Worth / Total Balance Worksheet and your experience will be much closer to an online banking experience.*

Fun Money Fact

If you stacked $1 bills one-mile high, you would have over $14 million.

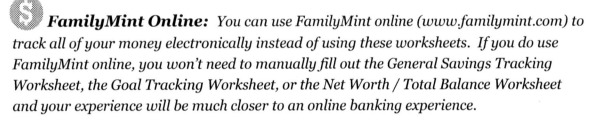

Note:

- For additional worksheets and forms, go to

  familymint.com/forms

EXAMPLE

General Savings Tracking Worksheet

NAME:	General Savings

General Savings is used to track money that you are not already tracking on a particular goal worksheet. This is money that is "left over" or money that you just haven't decided what to do with yet. For example, if your parents provide you an allowance or interest, you may choose to enter it here first, and then later transfer a portion of it to a particular goal.

Picture:

DATE	DESCRIPTION	SUBTRACTIONS Amount of Payment or Withdrawal (-)	ADDITIONS Amount of Deposit or Interest (+)	BALANCE
11/2	Starting Balance		$75.00	$75.00
11/7	Go to movies with friends	$10.00		$65.00
11/15	New video game	$35.00		$30.00
11/20	Gift from Aunt Karen		$25.00	$55.00
11/23	Allowance money		$2.00	$57.00
11/23	Clean house after Thanksgiving		$3.00	$60.00
11/23	Transfer to Goal: Mom's Present	$2.00		$58.00
11/25	Milkshake	$3.50		$54.50
12/1	Nerf gun	$23.00		$31.50
12/2	New fish	$5.00		$26.50
12/7	Allowance money		$2.00	$28.50
12/8	Babysitting		$45.00	$73.50

General Savings Tracking Worksheet

NAME:	General Savings

General Savings is used to track money that you are not already tracking on a particular goal worksheet. This is money that is "left over" or money that you just haven't decided what to do with yet. For example, if your parents provide you an allowance or interest, you may choose to enter it here first, and then later transfer a portion of it to a particular goal.

If you need help, refer back to Example on the left.

Picture:

DATE	DESCRIPTION	SUBTRACTIONS Amount of Payment or Withdrawal (-)	ADDITIONS Amount of Deposit or Interest (+)	BALANCE

General Savings Tracking Worksheet

Tracking
Workshe

NAME:	General Savings

DATE	DESCRIPTION	SUBTRACTIONS Amount of Payment or Withdrawal (-)	ADDITIONS Amount of Deposit or Interest (+)	BALANCE

Use additional worksheets if you run out of space.

EXAMPLE

Goal Tracking Worksheet

GOAL NAME:	Mom's birthday present
COST ($):	$20.00
Reach Goal By (date):	December 8
Weeks Remaining:	5
Weekly Target ($): (Cost ÷ Weeks remaining)	$4.00

Picture:

DATE	DESCRIPTION	SUBTRACTIONS Amount of Payment or Withdrawal (-)	ADDITIONS Amount of Deposit or Interest (+)	BALANCE	Progress % (Balance ÷ cost)
11/5	Mowing grass		$5.00	$5.00	25%
11/9	Allowance money		$2.00	$7.00	35%
11/17	Washed cars		$4.00	$11.00	55%
11/23	Transfer from General Savings		$2.00	$13.00	65%
11/26	Mowing grass		$5.00	$18.00	90%
12/2	Dusting miniblinds		$2.00	$20.00	100%!!
12/5	Buy mom's present	$20.00		$0.00	

To calculate Progress %, divide the Balance by the Cost. For example, in row 1, the current Balance is $5.00 and the Cost of the goal is $20.00. So, $5.00 ÷ $20.00 = .25, or 25%.

If you need help, refer back to the example.

GOAL NAME:	
COST ($):	
Reach Goal By (date):	
Weeks Remaining:	
Weekly Target ($): (Cost ÷ Weeks remaining)	

Picture:

DATE	DESCRIPTION	SUBTRACTIONS Amount of Payment or Withdrawal (-)	ADDITIONS Amount of Deposit or Interest (+)	BALANCE	Progress % (Balance ÷ Cost)

Goal Tracking Worksheet - *Goal #1*

GOAL NAME:	

DATE	DESCRIPTION	SUBTRACTIONS Amount of Payment or Withdrawal (-)	ADDITIONS Amount of Deposit or Interest (+)	BALANCE	Progress % (Balance ÷ cost)

Use additional worksheets if you run out of space.

FamilyMint Money Management Certification Prog

If you need help, refer back to the example.

GOAL NAME:	
COST ($):	
Reach Goal By (date):	
Weeks Remaining:	
Weekly Target ($): (Cost ÷ Weeks remaining)	

Picture:

DATE	DESCRIPTION	SUBTRACTIONS Amount of Payment or Withdrawal (-)	ADDITIONS Amount of Deposit or Interest (+)	BALANCE	Progress % (Balance ÷ Cost)

Goal Tracking Worksheet - *Goal #2*

GOAL NAME:

DATE	DESCRIPTION	SUBTRACTIONS Amount of Payment or Withdrawal (-)	ADDITIONS Amount of Deposit or Interest (+)	BALANCE	Progress % (Balance ÷ Cost)

Use additional worksheets if you run out of space.

FamilyMint Money Management Certification Prog

Goal Tracking Worksheet - *Goal #3*

If you need help, refer back to the example.

GOAL NAME:	
COST ($):	
Reach Goal By (date):	
Weeks Remaining:	
Weekly Target ($): (Cost ÷ Weeks remaining)	

Picture:

DATE	DESCRIPTION	SUBTRACTIONS Amount of Payment or Withdrawal (-)	ADDITIONS Amount of Deposit or Interest (+)	BALANCE	Progress % (Balance ÷ Cost)

GOAL NAME:

DATE	DESCRIPTION	SUBTRACTIONS Amount of Payment or Withdrawal (-)	ADDITIONS Amount of Deposit or Interest (+)	BALANCE	Progress % (Balance ÷ Goal)

Use additional worksheets if you run out of space.

If you need help, refer back to the example.

GOAL NAME:	
COST ($):	
Reach Goal By (date):	
Weeks Remaining:	
Weekly Target ($): (Cost ÷ Weeks remaining)	

Picture:

DATE	DESCRIPTION	SUBTRACTIONS Amount of Payment or Withdrawal (-)	ADDITIONS Amount of Deposit or Interest (+)	BALANCE	Progress % (Balance ÷ Cost)

Goal Tracking Worksheet - *Goal #4*

	GOAL NAME:				

DATE	DESCRIPTION	SUBTRACTIONS Amount of Payment or Withdrawal (-)	ADDITIONS Amount of Deposit or Interest (+)	BALANCE	Progress % (Balance ÷ Cost)

Use additional worksheets if you run out of space.

FamilyMint Money Management Certification Progr

Net Worth Tracking Worksheet

Use this worksheet to track the total of all your money. Your money is spread out between General Savings and each of your Goal accounts, so use this worksheet to summarize and track the total of all your money. This Total Balance is also known as your Net Worth. *Update this worksheet once per week.*

DATE	General Savings	Goal #1	Goal #2	Goal #3	Goal #4	TOTAL BALANCE (=Net Worth)
11/2	$75.00					$75.00
11/9	$65.00	$7.00				$72.00
11/16	$30.00	$7.00				$37.00
11/23	$58.00	$13.00	$2.50			$71.00
11/30	$54.50	$18.00	$5.00	$1.00		$78.50
12/7	$28.50	$0	$7.50	$2.00		$38.00
12/14	$73.50		$10.00	$3.00		$86.50

Use this worksheet to track the total of all your money. Your money is spread out between General Savings and each of your Goal accounts, so use this worksheet to summarize and track the total of all your money. This Total Balance is also known as your Net Worth. Update this weekly. *If you need help, refer back to the example.*

DATE	General Savings	Goal #1	Goal #2	Goal #3	Goal #4	TOTAL BALANCE (=Net Worth)

Here's a sample check that has already been filled out. Refer back to the Tracking Your Money chapter for more detailed instructions.

Practice Checks
For instructional use only. No cash value.

Date _January 1, 2013_

PAY TO THE ORDER OF _Mega Toy Store_ $ _43.16_

Forty three and 16/100 _____ DOLLARS

MEMO _Roller blades_   _Jamie Smith_

Here's a sample deposit slip that has already been filled out. Refer back to the Tracking Your Money chapter for more detailed instructions.

Practice Deposit Slip
For instructional use only.

DATE _January 1, 2013_

Don't forget to endorse the back of your checks with your signature

CASH _10.00_

CHECKS _15.00_

_25.00_

TOTAL DEPOSIT _50.00_

Use these Practice Checks below for additional practice in check writing.

Practice Checks
For instructional use only. No cash value.

Date _____

PAY TO THE
ORDER OF _____ $ [   ]

_____ DOLLARS

MEMO _____ _____

Practice Checks
For instructional use only. No cash value.

Date _____

PAY TO THE
ORDER OF _____ $ [   ]

_____ DOLLARS

MEMO _____ _____

Practice Checks
For instructional use only. No cash value.

Date _____

PAY TO THE
ORDER OF _____ $ [   ]

_____ DOLLARS

MEMO _____ _____

Checks

Endorse Here

X

Back of check

Endorse Here

X

Back of check

Endorse Here

X

Back of check

Use these Practice Checks below for additional practice in check writing.

Practice Checks
For instructional use only. No cash value.

Date _____

PAY TO THE
ORDER OF _____ $ [_____]

_____ DOLLARS

MEMO _____ _____

Practice Checks
For instructional use only. No cash value.

Date _____

PAY TO THE
ORDER OF _____ $ [_____]

_____ DOLLARS

MEMO _____ _____

Practice Checks
For instructional use only. No cash value.

Date _____

PAY TO THE
ORDER OF _____ $ [_____]

_____ DOLLARS

MEMO _____ _____

Endorse Here

X

Back of check

Endorse Here

X

Back of check

Endorse Here

X

Back of check

Deposit Slips

Use these Practice Deposit Slips for additional practice in writing deposit slips.

Practice Deposit Slip
For instructional use only.

DATE _____

SIGNATURE _____

CASH

CHECKS

TOTAL DEPOSIT

Practice Deposit Slip
For instructional use only.

DATE _____

SIGNATURE _____

CASH

CHECKS

TOTAL DEPOSIT

Practice Deposit Slip
For instructional use only.

DATE _____

SIGNATURE _____

CASH

CHECKS

TOTAL DEPOSIT

Deposit Slips

Back of Deposit Slip

Back of Deposit Slip

Back of Deposit Slip

Deposit Slips

Use these Practice Deposit Slips for additional practice in writing deposit slips.

Practice Deposit Slip
For instructional use only.

DATE _____

SIGNATURE _____

CASH

CHECKS

TOTAL DEPOSIT

Practice Deposit Slip
For instructional use only.

DATE _____

SIGNATURE _____

CASH

CHECKS

TOTAL DEPOSIT

Practice Deposit Slip
For instructional use only.

DATE _____

SIGNATURE _____

CASH

CHECKS

TOTAL DEPOSIT

Deposit Slips

Back of Deposit Slip

Back of Deposit Slip

Back of Deposit Slip

Practice check exercise - page 10

Practice Checks
For instructional use only. No cash value.

Date _Today's Date_

PAY TO THE ORDER OF _Shoe World_ $ 27.45

Twenty Seven and 45/100 DOLLARS

MEMO _Shoes_ _Your Signature_

Practice deposit slip exercise - page 11

Practice Deposit Slip
For instructional use only.

DATE _Today's Date_

Don't forget to endorse the back of your checks with your signature.

CASH	25.00
CHECKS	10.00
	30.00
	20.00
TOTAL DEPOSIT	85.00

Vocabulary matching exercise - page 11

- Transactions
- Money Management
- Income
- Register
- Check
- Deposit
- Endorse
- Withdrawal

- A written record of items, names or actions
- Adding or placing money into an account
- A form of payment that is withdrawn from your account
- The placing of one's signature on a document
- Process of tracking income, savings and spending
- Taking money out of an account
- The act of receiving or giving, buying or selling
- Money received

Envelope exercise - page 19

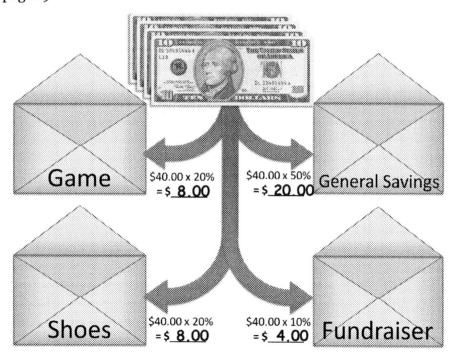

Game $40.00 x 20% = $ _8.00_

General Savings $40.00 x 50% = $ _20.00_

Shoes $40.00 x 20% = $ _8.00_

Fundraiser $40.00 x 10% = $ _4.00_

Answer Key

1. Simple interest exercise - page 23

    (a) Calculate the answer using the simple interest formula:

        Simple Interest = $500 x .10 x 5 = **$250**

    (b) Calculate the answer using the table:

Principal = $500	Current Balance	Interest Paid = 10%	Principal + Interest
Year 1	$ 500	$ 50	$ 550
Year 2	$ 550	$ 50	$ 600
Year 3	$ 600	$ 50	$ 650
Year 4	$ 650	$ 50	$ 700
Year 5	$ 700	$ 50	$ 750
	Total Int.	$ 250	

2. Compound interest exercise - page 23 - 24

    (a) Calculate the answer using the compound interest formula:

        Compound Interest = $[\$500 \times (1 + 0.10)^5] - 500$

                = [$500 x (1.10 x 1.10 x 1.10 x 1.10 x 1.10)] - $500

                = ($500 x 1.6105) - $500

                = **$305.25**

    (b) Calculate the answer using the table:

Principal = $500	Current Balance	Interest Paid = 10%	Principal + Interest
Year 1	$ 500.00	$ 50.00	$ 550.00
Year 2	$ 550.00	$ 55.00	$ 605.00
Year 3	$ 605.00	$ 60.50	$ 665.50
Year 4	$ 665.50	$ 66.55	$ 732.05
Year 5	$ 732.05	$ 73.20	$ 805.25
	Total Int.	$ 305.25	

3. How much more did you earn with compound interest as compared to simple interest? **$55.25**

ONLINE!

familymint.com/yflfoundation

Your FamilyMint Premium Online Access Includes:

✓ Ability to complete all Certification Program activities online

✓ Create goals and see progress toward achieving each of them

✓ Track money coming in and going out

✓ Create a Savings Plan that automates "envelope system" deposits

✓ Mobile application access at m.familymint.com

✓ Lifetime software access included. No ongoing monthly or annual fees

✓ and much more!

Parent/Guardian: Visit **familymint.com/yflfoundation** to sign up and start using FamilyMint Premium online today!

Brought to you by:

YFLFoundation.org

Parent Checklist

Use this checklist prior to signing the certificate

Verify that your child:

☐ Completed all the exercises in the front chapters of this workbook.

☐ Tracked all their money coming in and going out for at least two months in either this workbook or FamilyMint online.

☐ Created at least three goals.

☐ Achieved at least one goal.

☐ Practiced writing at least three checks.

☐ Practiced writing at least three deposit slips.

☐ Completed the Learning Summary section.

To complete the assignment:

☐ Ensure all boxes are checked on this page and you've signed below.

☐ Sign the certificate on the back cover with a ball point pen where indicated.

☐ Celebrate your child's accomplishment!

Parent / Guardian signature: _____